for:
Charlotte
& Graham,
love Daddy

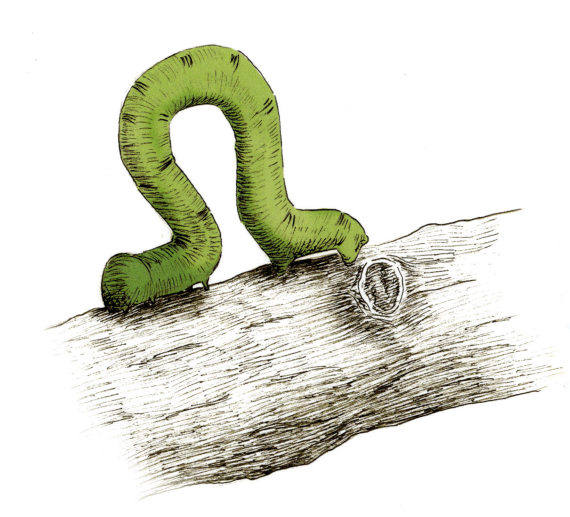

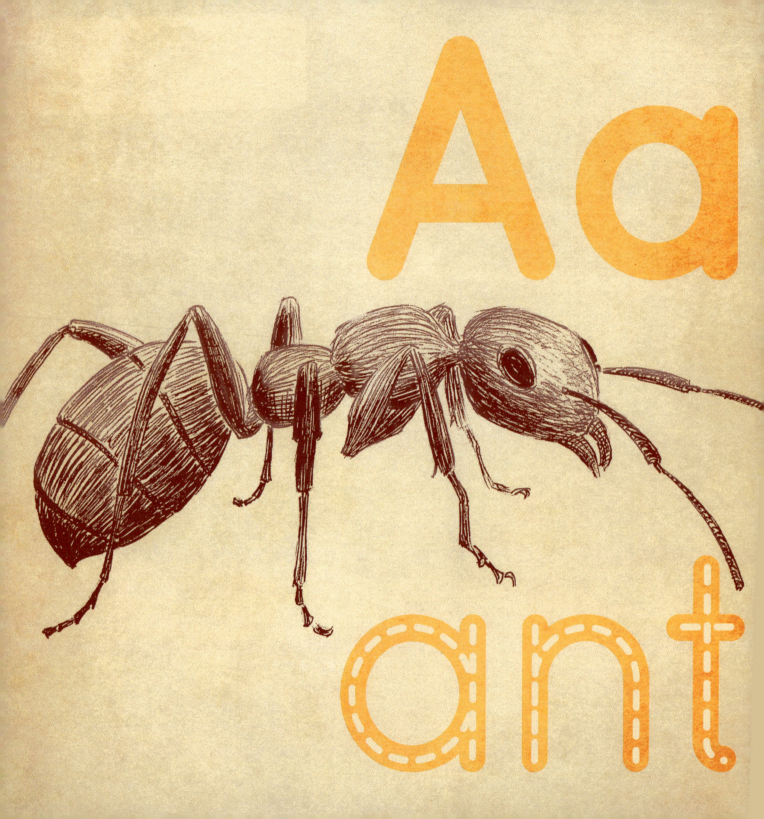

blue jay

Bb

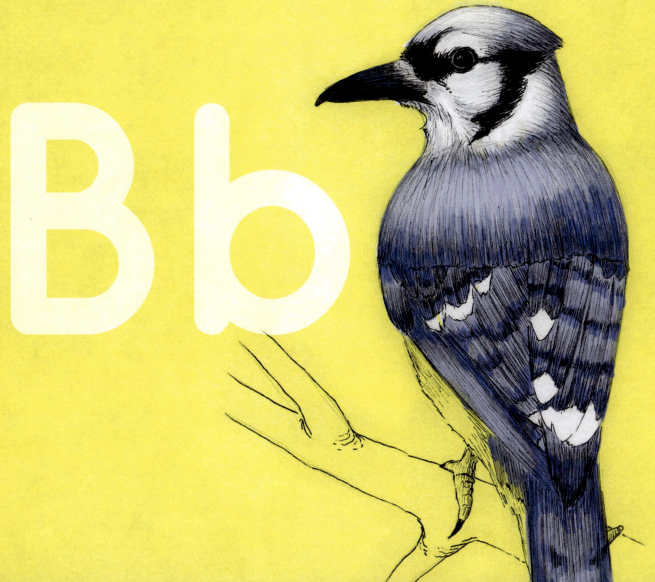

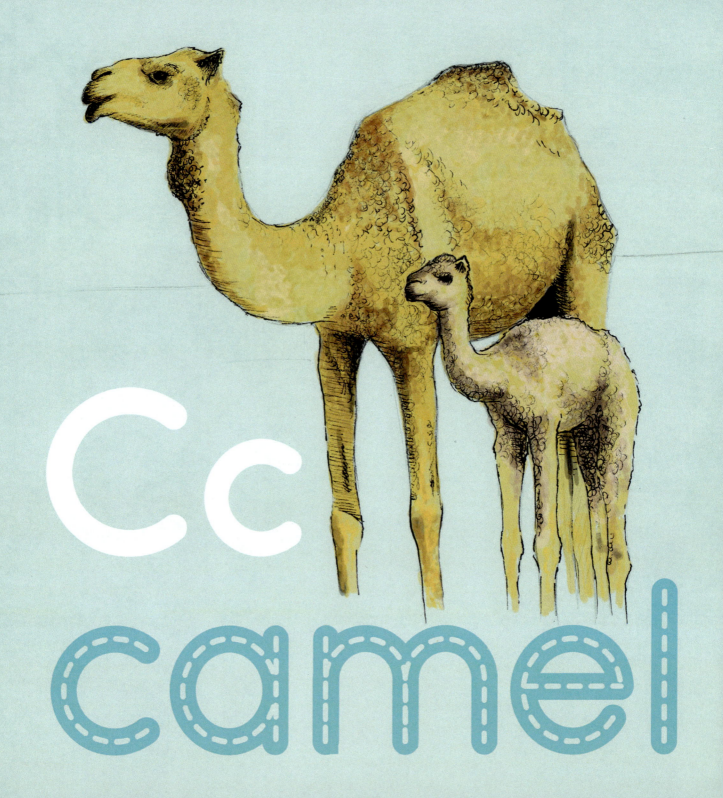

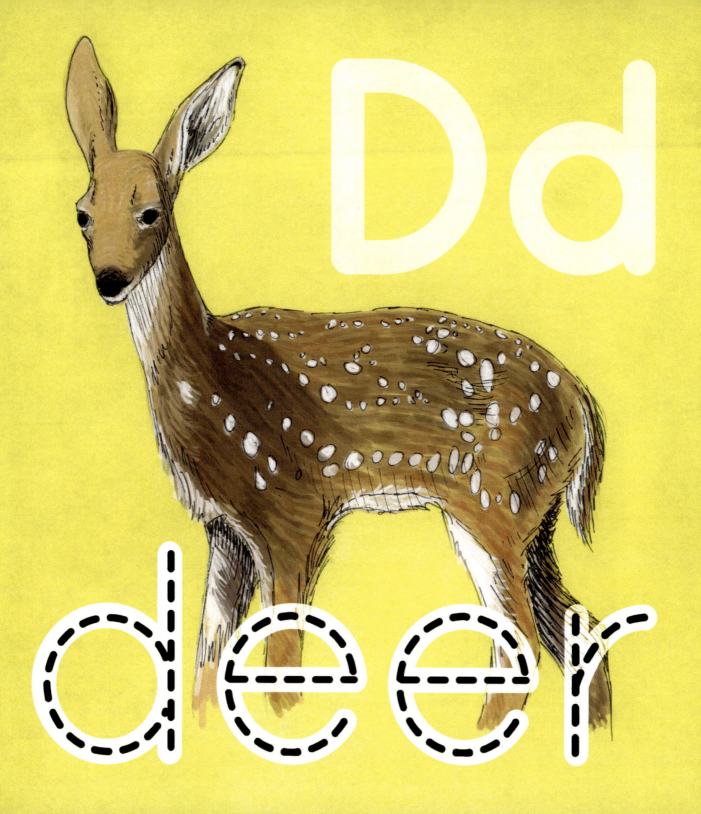

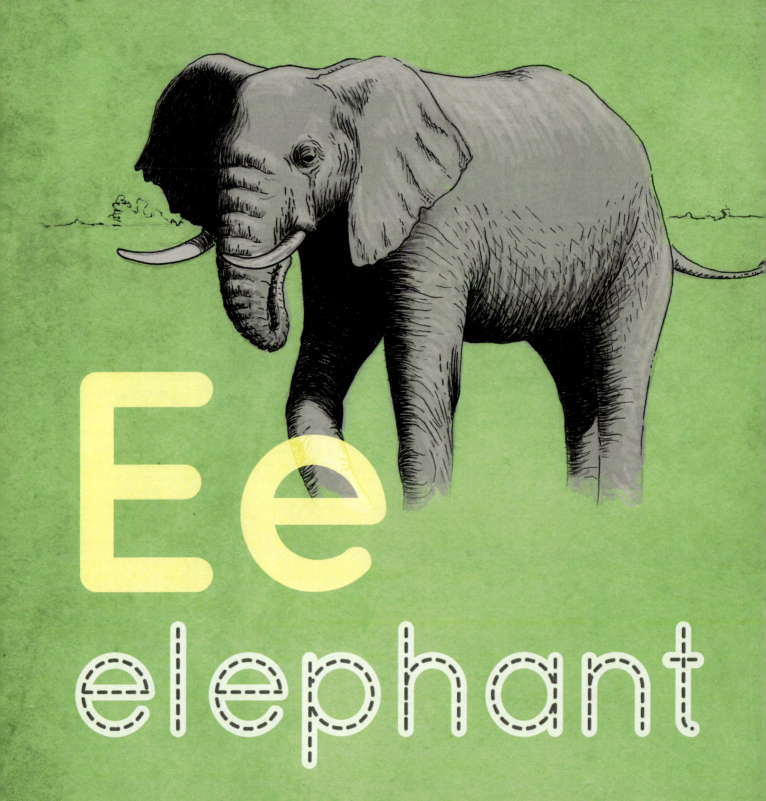

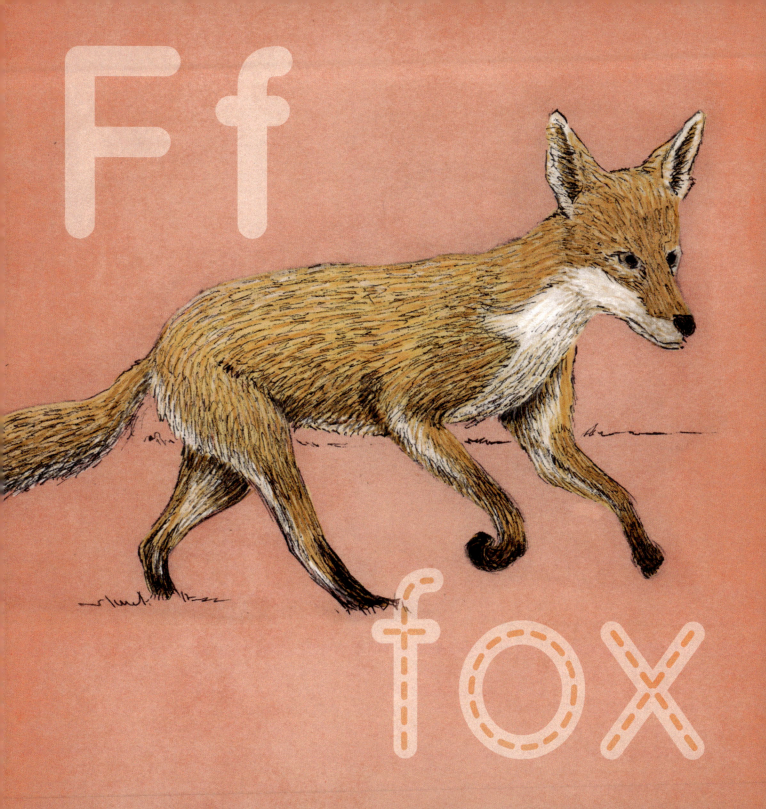

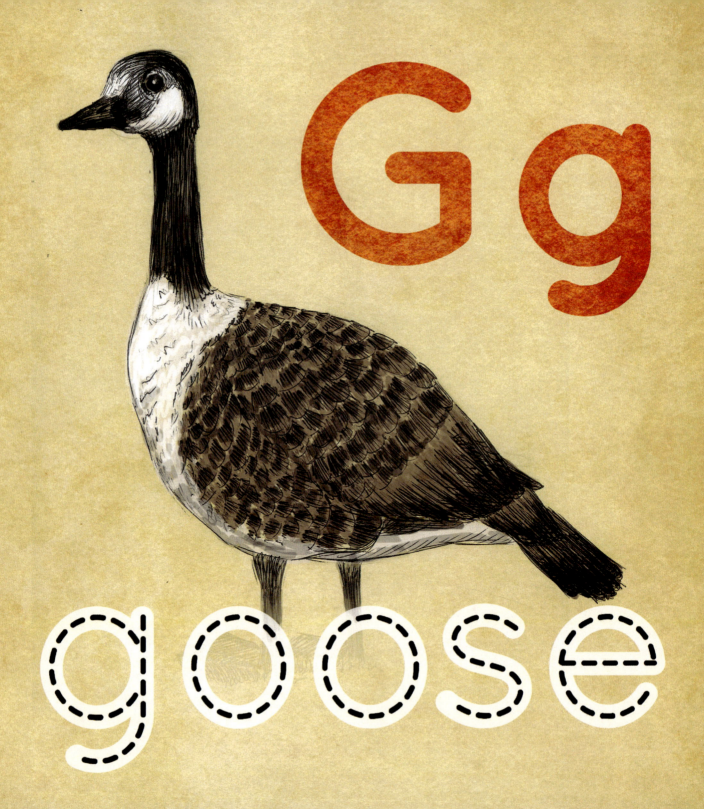

hummingbird

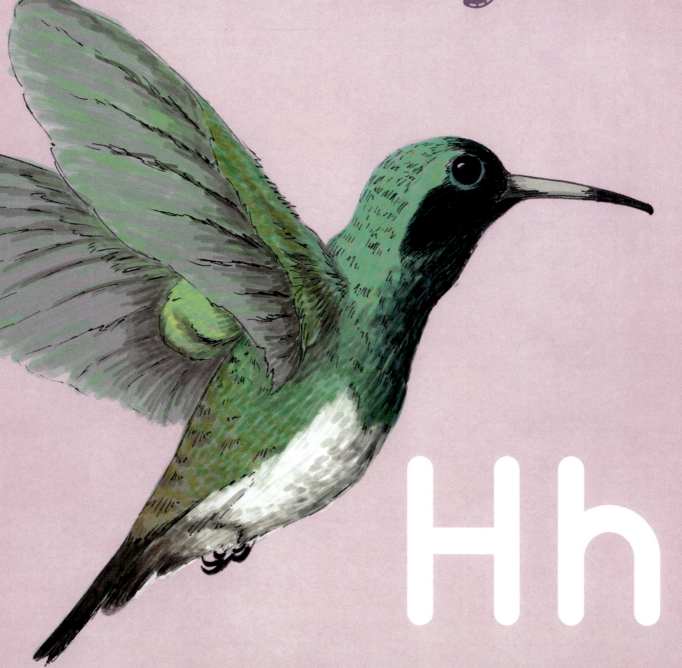

Hh

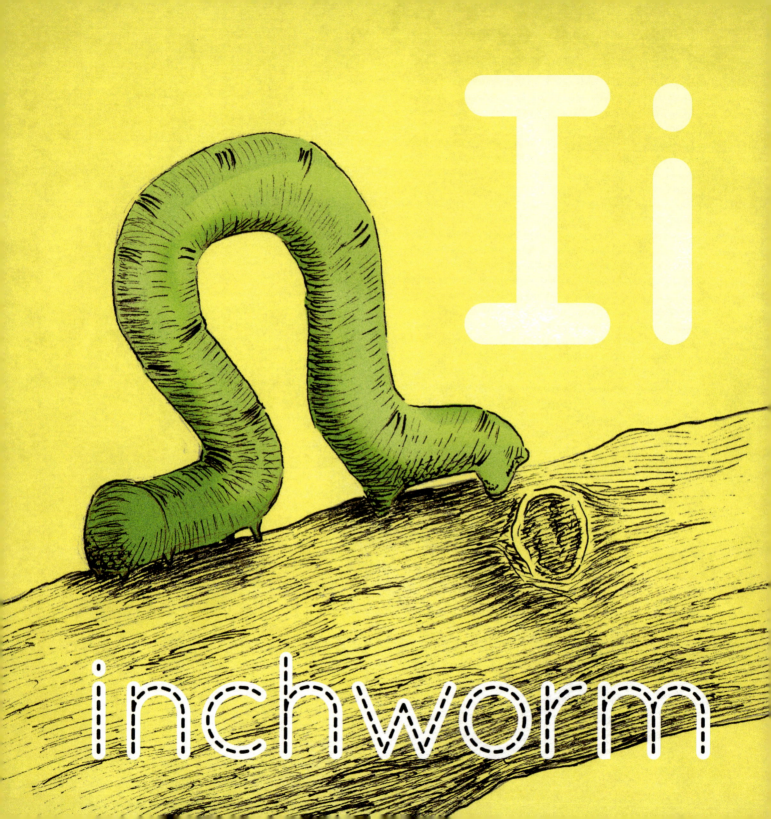

jellyfish

Jj

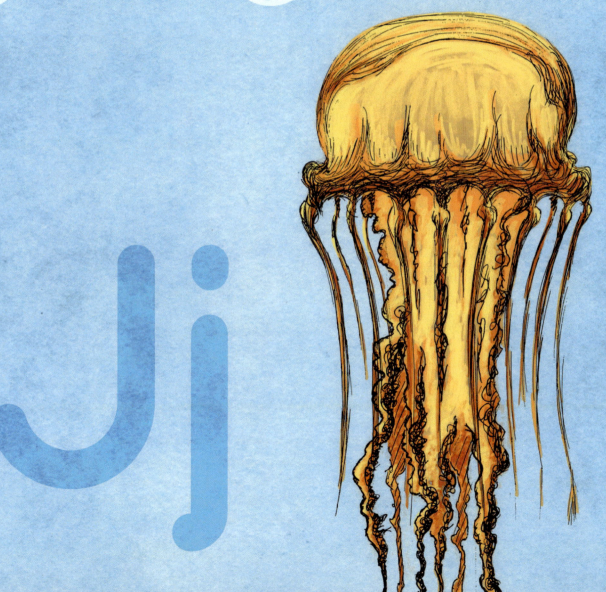

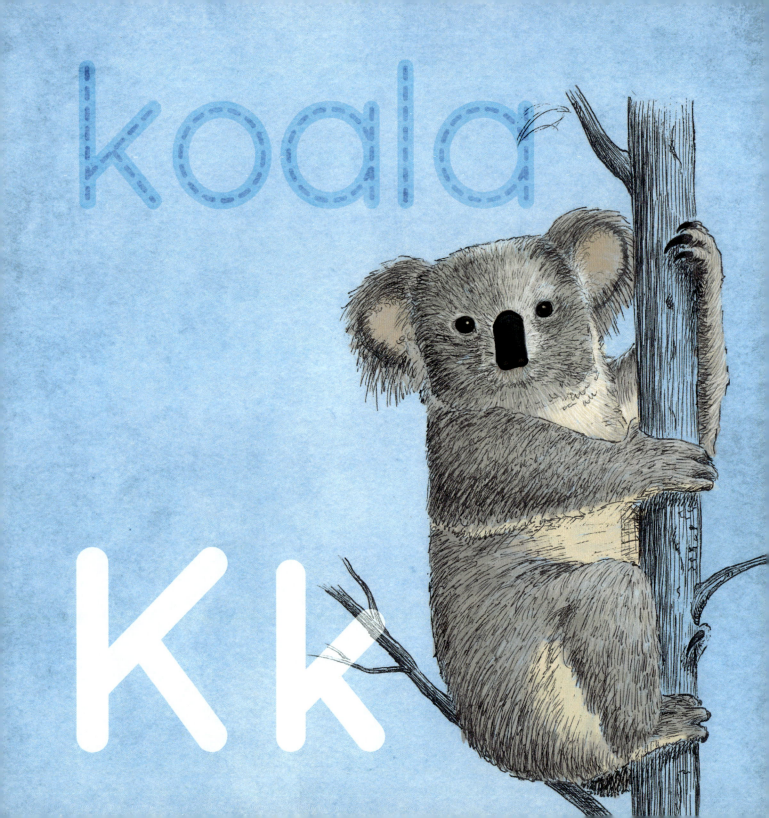

lizard

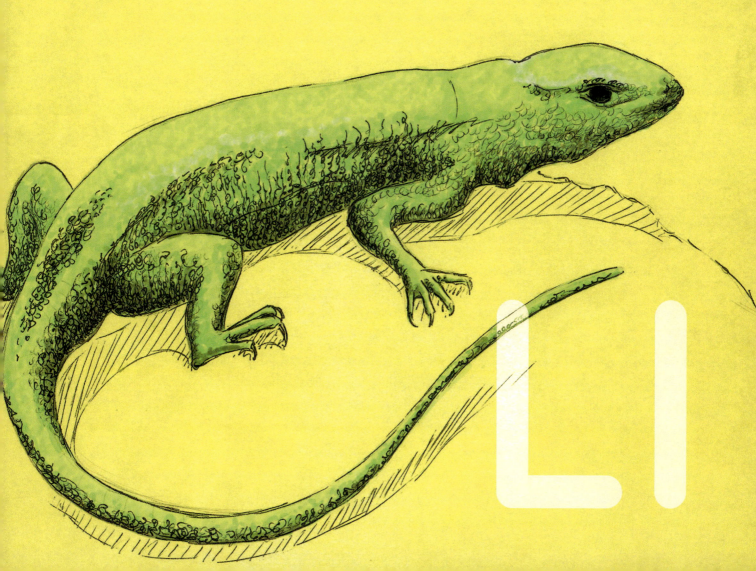

Ll

moose

Mm

Nn
narwhal

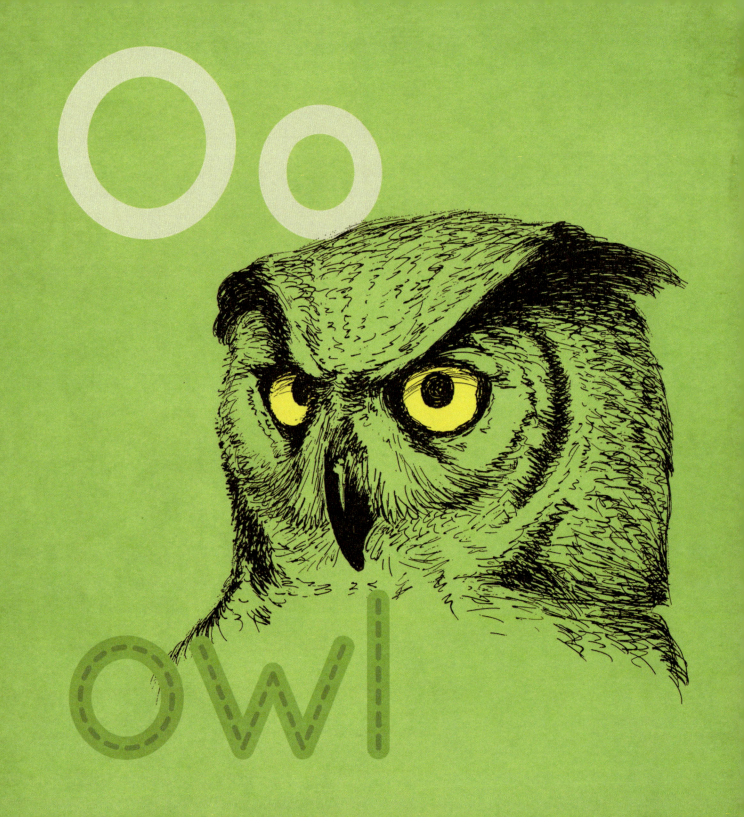

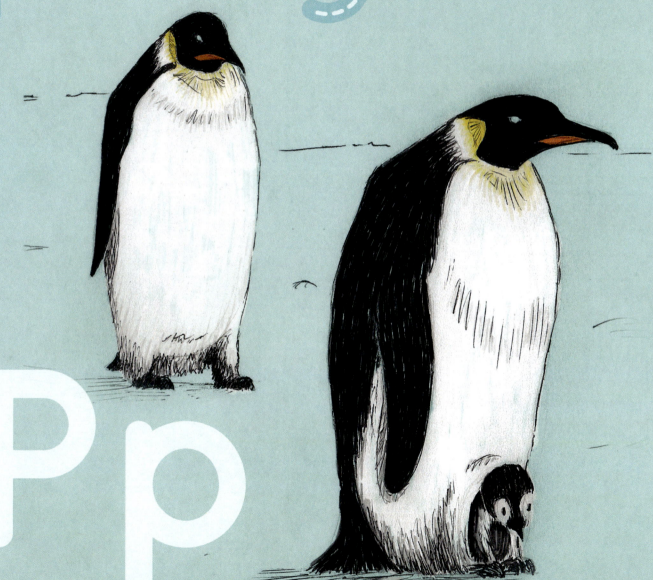

penguin

Pp

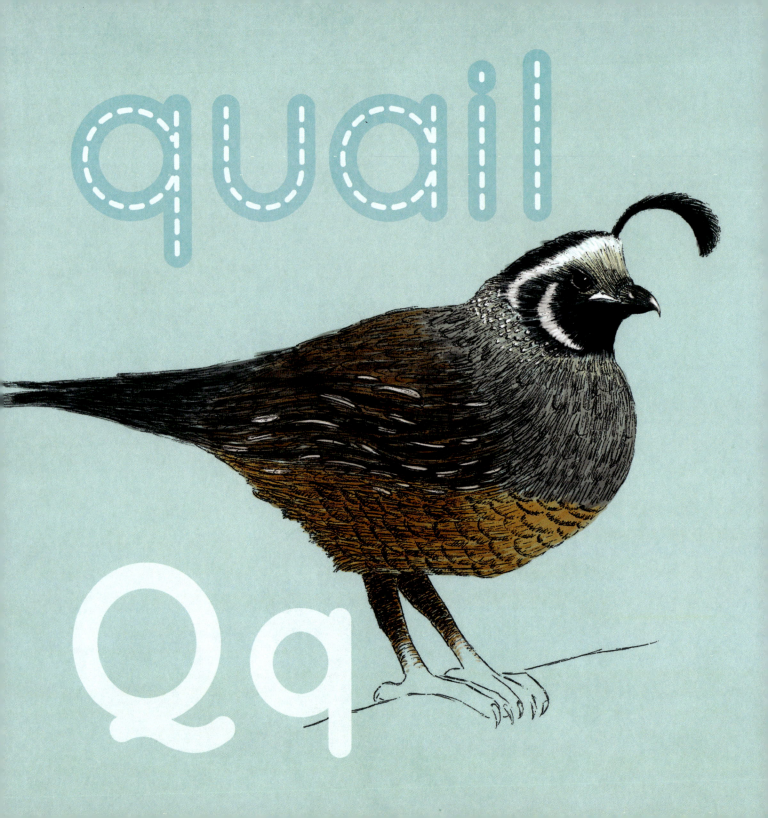

Rr

rabbit

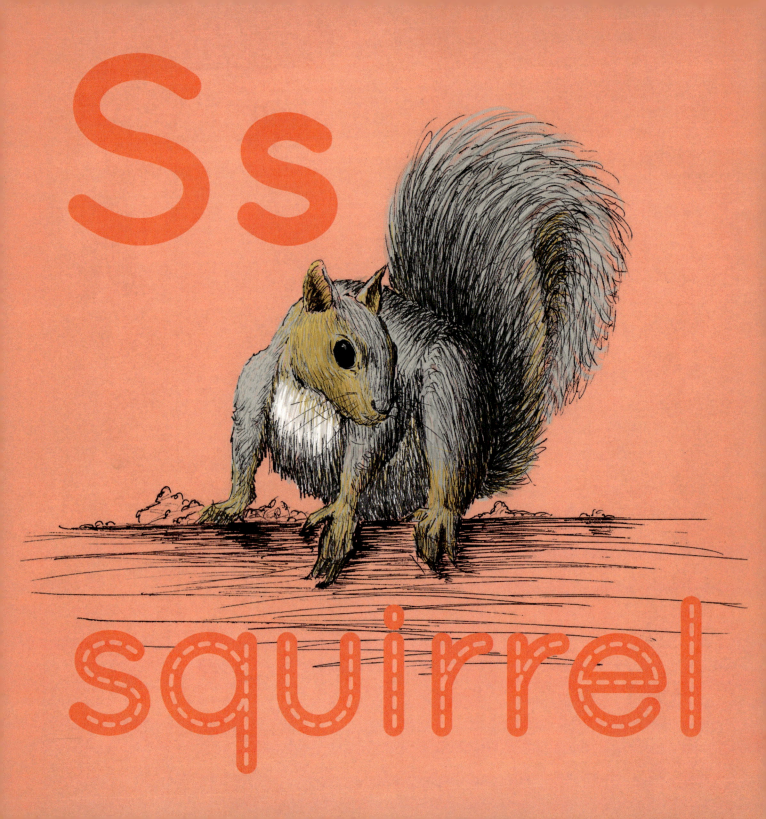

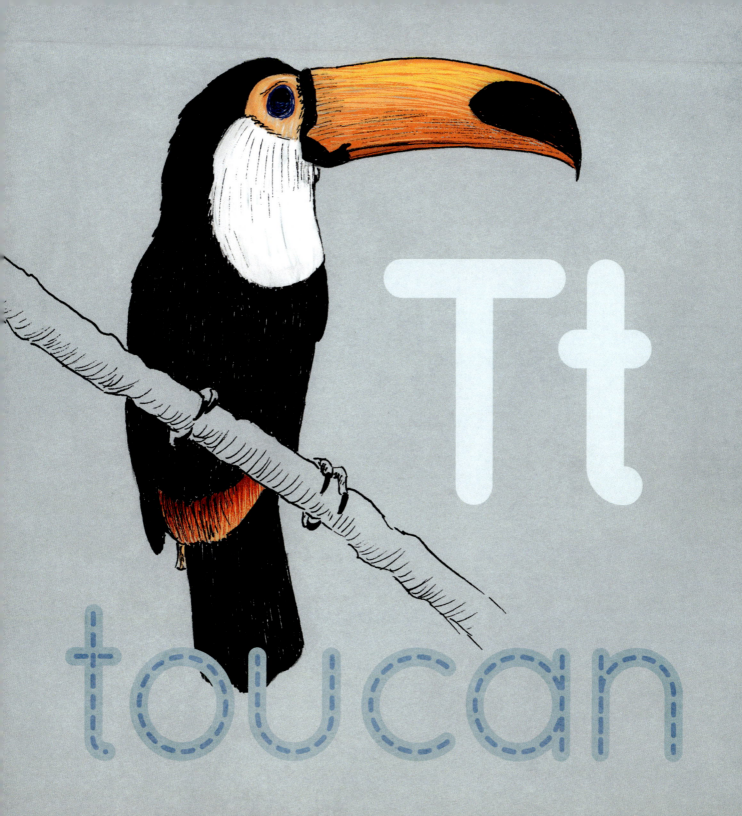

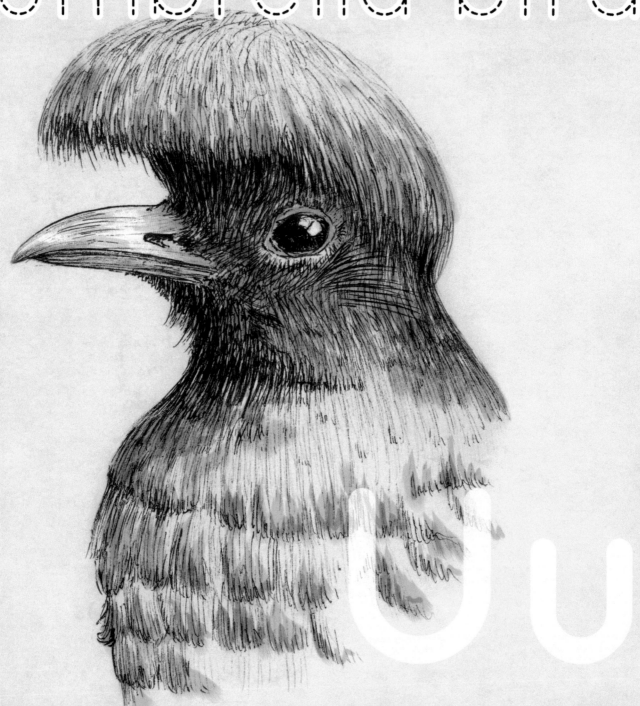

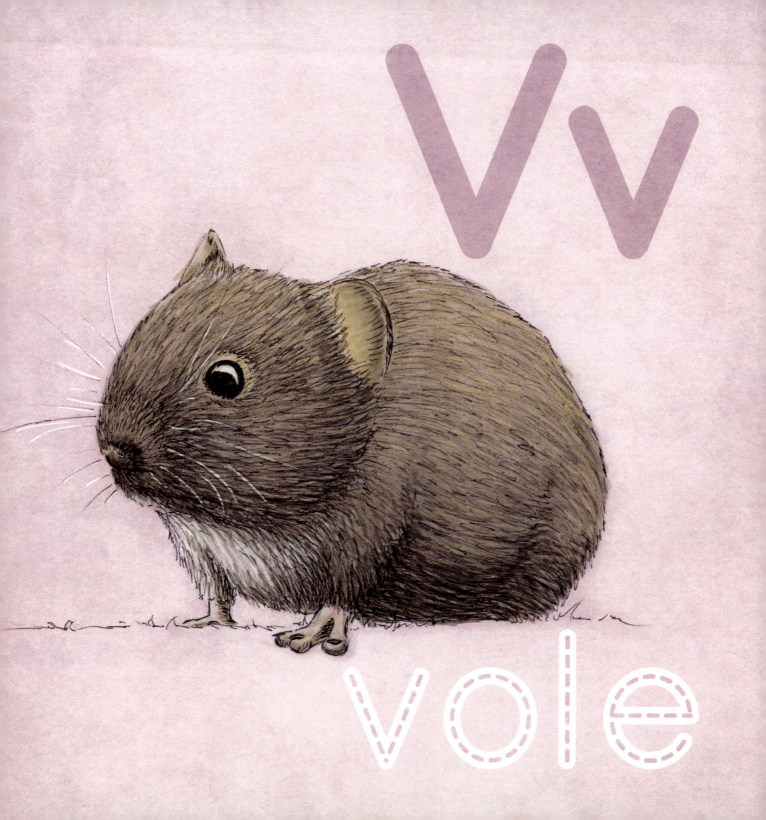

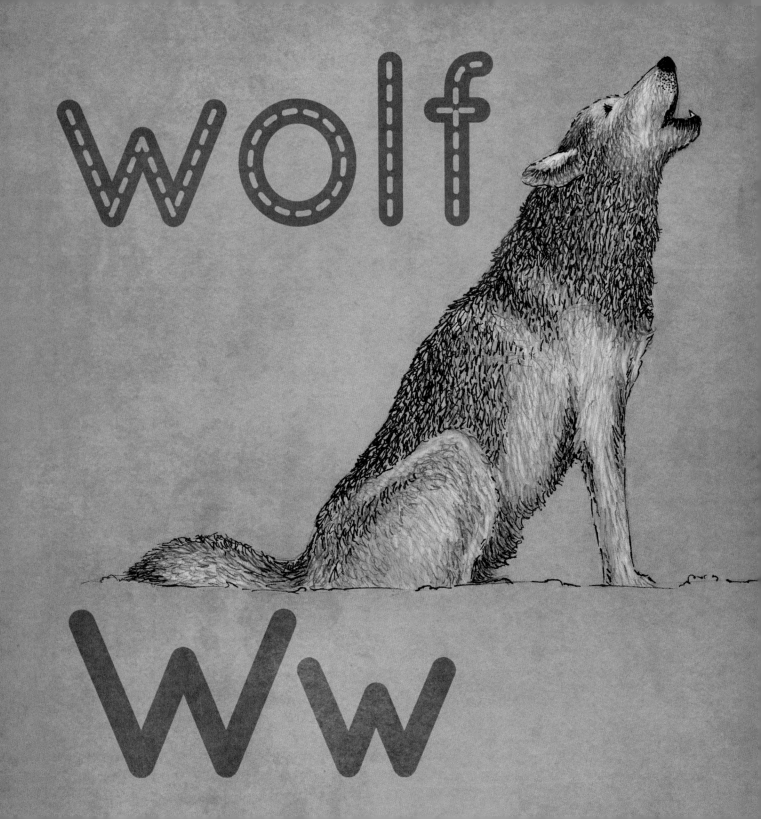

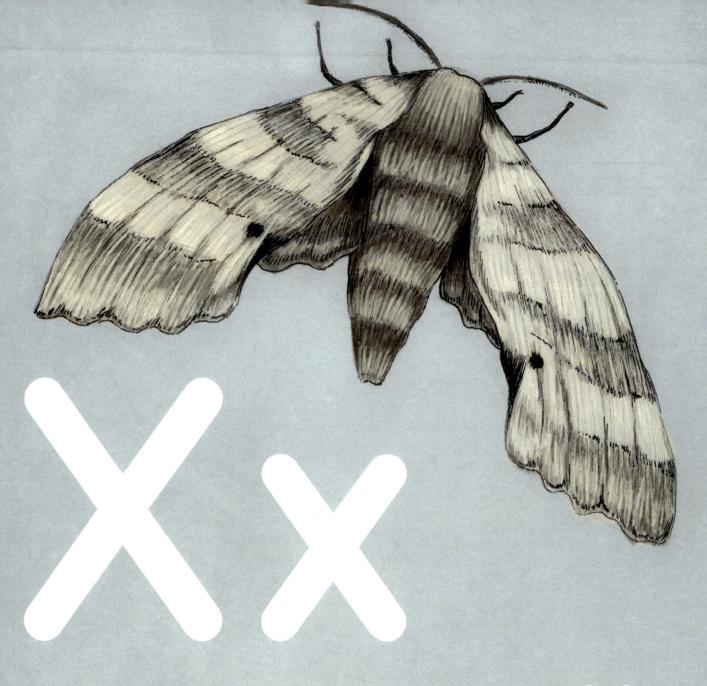

Xx
xoona moth

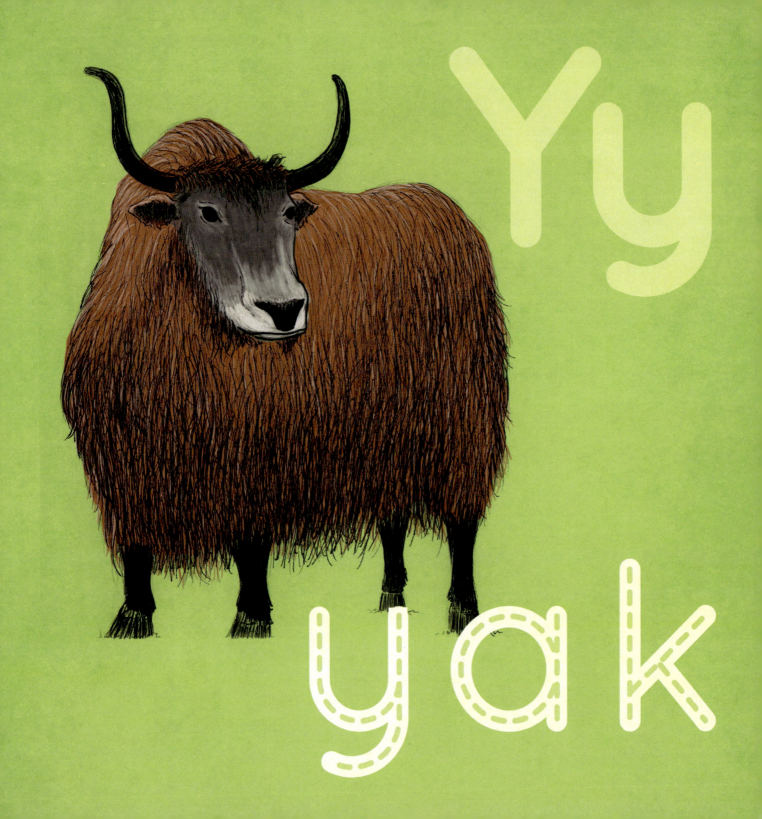

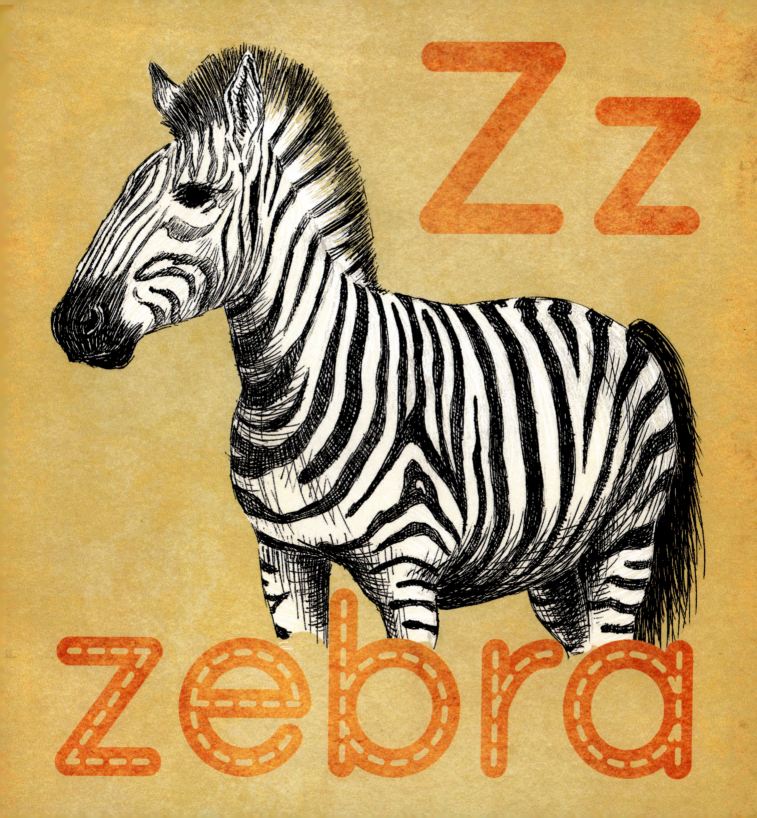

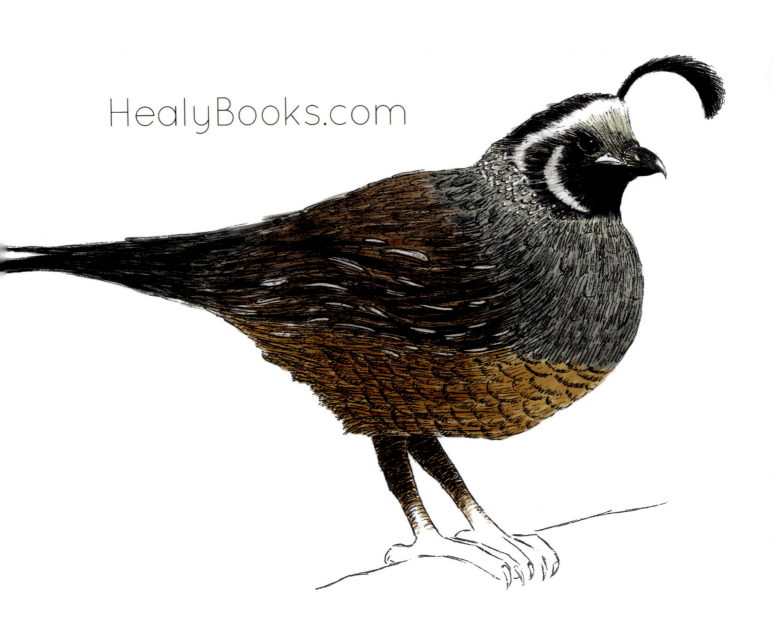

Made in the USA
Las Vegas, NV
19 November 2021